How Winning the Lottery Changed My Life

How Winning the Lottery Changed My Life

WINDFALL: A BLESSING OR A CURSE?

Sandra Hayes

AuthorHouse™
1663 Liberty Drive
Bloomington, IN 47403
www.authorhouse.com
Phone: 1-800-839-8640

© 2011 by Sandra Hayes. All rights reserved.

No part of this book may be reproduced, stored in a retrieval system, or transmitted by any means without the written permission of the author.

First published by AuthorHouse   11/08/2011

ISBN: 978-1-4678-7046-7 (sc)
ISBN: 978-1-4678-7044-3 (ebk)

Library of Congress Control Number: 2011960489

Printed in the United States of America

Any people depicted in stock imagery provided by Thinkstock are models, and such images are being used for illustrative purposes only.
Certain stock imagery © Thinkstock.

Because of the dynamic nature of the Internet, any web addresses or links contained in this book may have changed since publication and may no longer be valid. The views expressed in this work are solely those of the author and do not necessarily reflect the views of the publisher, and the publisher hereby disclaims any responsibility for them.

Chapter 1

ANTICIPATION

On December 5, 2007, my fiancé Charles and I were sitting on the sofa in my den watching television. We were anxiously waiting to watch the reality show *Million Dollar Christmas*, which was a two-part show that featured four out of the thirteen winners of the April 2006 Missouri Powerball drawing. I was going to be featured on part two of the show.

While watching the show, I was disappointed with how they told my story. The reason for my disappointment was that the show was supposed to contain heartfelt and heartwarming stories about our first Christmas as Millionaires. At least that's what the executive producers pitched when they sold us the idea for the show. It was that pitch and the producers' warmth that made me want to do the show. I wanted the experience of making a reality show, and I wanted to make my friends and family, who were a part of my life, a part of this reality show.

Even though my fiancé Charles loved the show, I was disappointed with how it had turned out. They had turned my story into something controversial. It was not heartwarming. I did not like some of the issues the show focused on.

Of the four stories, mine seemed to get the biggest reaction from the public. I received both positive and negative feedback from people across the United States.

In this book, I will tell you about the love I received and the hate, the hopes, and the regrets that come with a life-altering change. After reading this book, perhaps you will be able to answer this question. Is winning the lottery a blessing or a curse?

Chapter 2

THE STORM

One day in early March 2006, I was really down. I was feeling tired, not just physically tired, but emotionally and spiritually. I admit it—I was really feeling sorry for myself.

I was scared about finances. Scared because I was about to complete my second master's degree. My yearly salary was not enough to pay back the loan without going into debt. Even though I had a job that I loved, I was making less than $26 thousand a year. I was worried because I knew I would have to work two jobs in order to pay off my student loans. Due to my health problems, I felt that I could not work a second job. I have discoid lupus, a chronic illness.

I was diagnosed with lupus in 2005. Lupus is a chronic illness that can affect your organs, muscles, and joints. Lupus often mimics other illnesses, making you believe, for example, that you have the flu when in fact you do not. When you get sick, you really get sick. I also experience involuntary muscle spasms, which are very embarrassing. My lupus symptoms are worse in the winter. Coldness is my enemy. I have to be in a warm environment.

Stress also triggers episodes of lupus. In 2006, I was under a lot of stress and I was sick a lot. I often prayed that my lupus would go away. Because of this chronic illness, I would often miss work or come in late. This is the reason I felt I could not work a second job. How many employers would work with me when I was experiencing a lupus episode?

In addition to my financial worries, I was a divorcée and had no relationship or husband to help carry the weight. I wanted the Lord to bless me with someone who was real, who was my friend. I prayed for a man who would truly love me for who I was. I wanted a man who would appreciate me—a man who would stand by my side through sickness and in health.

God listens and does answers prayers.

That day, I had a long talk with the Lord and I stated my case to him. I thanked him for my home. I thanked him for helping me raise my children as a divorced, single mother. I thanked him for blessing me with my job.

My job at the time allowed me to help many people—children and families—but I reminded the Lord that I had unsuccessfully tried to get a promotion at work and had even applied for better paying jobs, both within the state government and with various employers. I told the Lord that I knew he loved me and had the best in store for me. *Man may let me down, but you, God, have always had my back.* Please help me. I thank you. Amen. I poured out my heart to God and rested my case. I needed a financial blessing. Little did I know the Lord had a reason for keeping me right there at that job.

I realized that day that you have to be grateful for the things you have in life. I have had many positive people in my life who love me and are very supportive of me. Some of those people are gone now but not forgotten. I truly miss them.

After I poured out my heart to God, I felt relieved, and I actually felt better. My spirit was lifted.

The truth was always within me. All my life, I have been strong and a fighter. For example, I used to be active in the union as a shop steward, at both the state level and the federal level. I have never been afraid to stand up for my rights or the rights of others.

My lupus did not stop me from working a second job to pay back my student loan. That's what a strong person does: she makes lemonade from lemons.

Chapter 3

THE SWEET RAY OF LIGHT

In the second week of March 2006; a coworker told me that people in my office were pooling their money together to play the lottery and asked me to join them. I was surprised because I had never been asked to participate before. Since no one had ever asked me if I wanted to play, I had to ask who was in charge of collecting the money. My coworker told me who was in charge and I went to him and told him that I wanted to join the lottery pool. He apologized to me for not having included me before, saying, "We forget about you being in the back." His cubicle was in another room in the front of the office, while mine was in the back. He assured me that the next time they played; he would make sure I was asked, too. He told me that the office only plays the lottery when the pot is big.

The next week, which was the third week of March 2006, I was sitting at my desk eating my lunch when I was asked by a coworker if I wanted to play the lottery. I said, "Yes", and handed the person one dollar, which I thought was the normal amount people played. My coworker who was collecting the money told me that everyone was putting in five dollars so we could buy lots of tickets. I gave him the five dollars to play and continued to eat my lunch.

Chapter 4

THE WINDFALL

It was Thursday morning, April 13, 2006. I normally watch the morning news while I am getting dressed for work. That morning, I was running late, so I did not watch the news. I normally left for work by 8:00 a.m. in order to arrive at work by 8:30. This particular morning I had overslept, so my regular morning routine was thrown off track. The clothes I had laid out to wear to work the night before were brand new, and I had not tried them on before buying them. To my surprise, they were too tight, but I did not have time to change into another outfit.

As I was combing my hair, my telephone rang. I thought about ignoring the call because I was running late, but I reluctantly answered the telephone. The caller was my supervisor. She apologized to me for calling my home and asked me what time I was coming in to work. She said she needed to talk to me. I felt a lump in my throat. My supervisor had never called my home before. I told her that I would be leaving my house in about five minutes. She said, "Okay," we said good-bye and hung up.

I was about to leave my home fifteen minutes later when my telephone rang again. I answered, "Hello?"

"You haven't left for work yet?" It was my supervisor again.

"I am leaving right now," I replied.

I was beginning to worry. I thought I had been laid off and was bracing myself to receive bad news. My supervisor anxiously said, "I have something to tell you." She then asked me to have a seat. She asked me if I was sitting down and I lied and told her, "Yes."

She then asked me if I had watched the news that morning. When I replied "no," she then told me I had won. I asked her, "Won? Won what?" I had no idea what she was talking about. She replied, *"The lottery!"*

I went completely numb. I was in a state of shock. I felt totally weak, like I was on a supernatural high. I was floating on cloud nine. I saw purple elephants flying past me, rainbows forming, and waterfalls falling. "Hello?" My supervisor interrupted my thoughts.

I said, "What?"

She said, "Did you hear what I just said to you?"

I replied, "Yes I did."

She then asked me was I still coming to work. I replied, "Yes I am."

Before I got out the door, my youngest daughter called me on my telephone. When I picked up she said, "Hi mom." Before

I could say hello, she asked me, "Did you know a group of social workers won the Powerball at your job?" She said, "My God, everyone at my job is talking about it."

When she got no reply, she asked, "Mom, did you play the Powerball yesterday?"

I replied, "Yes I did."

"You are kidding, right?"

I told my daughter, "No, I am not kidding."

She repeated, *"Mom? You're kidding."*

I told her again, "No baby, I am not kidding."

All I heard after that was my daughter screaming, *"We're rich! We're rich! We're rich! Um, I mean* you *are rich!"*

We hung up and almost immediately, the telephone rang again. This time when I answered, it was my best friend Pam, who was also my coworker. She said, "San, where are you?"

I replied, "I am trying to get to work."

She said, "San, don't you know that *you won the lottery?*"

"What?" I replied, "No!"

She said "You've got to be kidding, home girl."

I told her, "No, I am not kidding."

She then asked me, "Didn't you look at the news this morning?"

I innocently told her I hadn't. She then asked me if I wanted her to come over to my house to pick me up. She jokingly said that she would pick me for a hundred dollars. I told her no, thank you; I could drive myself to work. She then informed me that when I came to work that I would need to go into my office manager's office because the Lottery Commissioner was at the office waiting to meet the winners. So she commanded me, "Hurry up and get to work!"

I was halfway to work when my cell phone rang. it was Pam again asking me where I was. I said, "I am halfway there."

She responded, "They're all waiting for you; hurry up and get here".

"Okay!"

A few minutes later I pulled into the parking lot at work. I looked around and observed that the lot was unusually empty. I then got out of my car and entered the building.

I went through the entrance door and walked down the hall and through the employee entrance door. I was walking down an empty hall when suddenly the door to my department opened.

A group of my coworkers were running toward me, screaming loudly. They grabbed me and pulled me toward my cubicle. One of my coworkers began rubbing my back—she said it was for good luck—and another one pinched me.

Out of habit and disbelief, I immediately went into my cubicle to put my purse away. My girlfriend Pam came to my cubicle to escort me to the supervisor's office. My supervisor asked me very excitedly if I understood what was going on.

I told her, "No."

She then said, "I guess you think we are kidding?"

I told her, "Yes, I do." She then escorted me, along with my best friend, to my office manager's office.

When we arrived, my office manager had just gotten off the telephone. He was smiling and blushing. I believe he had tears of joy in his eyes. When I saw his reaction, I knew it was not a joke. At that point, a mix of emotions came over me. I remember a feeling of relief and excitement. Then feelings of euphoria hit me. At one point, I thought I was going to faint, but I did not.

Chapter 5

THE CLAIM

The winners who reported to work that day (a few of the lottery winners quit their jobs that day), were met by the Director of the Missouri Lottery in the office manager's office. That director informed us that there were reporters at Huck's, the convenience store where the ticket had been purchased. He said that they would be showing up at the office soon and that we needed to get away from that office as soon as possible. The lottery ticket had to be validated first.

Those of us who reported to work that day left the child support office and went to the attorney's office. I was still in a state of shock. I felt like a zombie. Fortunately, I did not have to drive to that attorney's office. I couldn't drive. I forgot how to. Luckily, one of the coworker lottery winners asked me to ride with her, and I did.

We had to have the winning ticket legally validated before we could let the news media know who the winners were. The person who had actually purchased the ticket was not at work that day. (I believe he quit his job.) He did, however, come to the office to let the lottery winners know that he had the winning ticket. He had kept it in a safe deposit box. As

I recall, that safe deposit box was located at his bank. His friend directed us to an attorney's office in Clayton for legal guidance. We were lucky because that attorney also hid us from the reporters who were on the hunt for those of us who knew about our windfall.

We stayed at the attorney's office until the winning lottery ticket was validated. The winners who were not at work showed up there. A representative of the Lottery Commission was also present.

What does "validate" mean? It means the Lottery Commission has to verify that the winning lottery ticket is real.

As we arrived at the attorney's office, we sat outside his conference room. We were waiting for the word to enter the conference room. I remember hearing many cell phones ringing, including mine. The win from the lottery had spread. One of my many cell phone calls, in particular, was from a former state employee who called to ask me if I had heard about the group of social workers who had won the lottery. I told her yes. She asked me if I knew who they were. I told her yes. She then asked who. I asked her to guess. She jokingly said, "You!" We were laughing as we hung up our phones.

Shortly thereafter, we were invited into the conference room where we met the attorney who would give us advice. Mind you, this advice did not come free. It was my understanding that this attorney had experience with clients who had windfalls of money. He was excellent at answering our questions and explaining our situation to us. The attorney told us what we could expect from people, how our lives would change, and how this windfall would affect our lives forever. We were also advised that if we did not spend our money wisely, we could go broke within a few years.

The Missouri Lottery Commission representative informed us that we had to make a decision as to whether we wanted to get our money in a lump sum or have a twenty-year installment payout. I chose the lump-sum payment. We completed paperwork that stated how we wanted to receive our winnings.

Within a few hours, the winning ticket was validated. No winner owed back child support, so no liens were attached to the claim. If you owe taxes or back child support, the government takes money from your winning portion before you receive your check.

We were then declared the official winners of the Missouri Power Ball. We had won $224 million dollars. We were dubbed "The Lucky Thirteen."

Actually, one ticket was split between two people who had bought their tickets together. As a result, they each received half of their winning portion. Guess what? When you win the lottery, you do not get all of the money that was won. The federal and state governments get their money from your winnings before you even get the money. Then the merchant who sold the winning ticket gets his cut.

I was told that I would ultimately receive more of my actual winnings if I took the annual payments for twenty years rather than taking a lump sum, but I chose to take the lump sum. Most of the winners also took the lump-sum payment, with the exception of one of the winners. As far as I know, we are all still comfortable. Some of us went to school to earn degrees, some started businesses, and others moved out of Missouri.

At the end of the winning year, the government takes, takes, and takes. I remember my hand sweating and shaking as I wrote checks to the federal and state governments to pay the additional taxes I was told I owed at the end of 2006.

Paying those taxes was mandatory. I was used to receiving refunds, not paying out large lump sums of money. I was not used to writing checks that large, but I was too scared not to pay what the federal and state governments said I had to pay. This is why I hired an investment firm, a broker, and an accountant to help manage my accounts.

After the lottery ticket was validated, it was time for the official presentation of the check by the lottery commission, which would be shown on live television. We were then escorted to a hotel. For the life of me, I cannot remember which hotel it was. This hotel provided us a huge conference room. The conference room was set up reception style and refreshments were provided. Also present in the conference room were the news reporters from many television stations and their camera personnel. The press interview is something that I will never forget.

Chapter 6

LIGHTS, CAMERA, ACTION

I will never forget feeling like a celebrity as we all walked down the red carpet. As we entered the room, people began clapping, and pictures were taken of us. All the local television stations and newspapers were there to get their story.

We were asked to go stand on the stage so pictures could be taken of us as we accepted a large symbolic check from the Missouri Lottery in the amount of $224,220,000. Our former office manager was asked to give a speech regarding our win. He was still blushing as he gave a speech about how it felt to win the lottery. I was still in a daze, and I felt as if I was in a dream. I remember that as I was standing on the stage and posing for pictures with the other winners, I made the comment out loud that I could not believe that this was happening. One of the Missouri Lottery Commission employees heard me when I said that. She looked at me, smiled, and then pinched me hard on my arm. She asked me, "Now do you believe you have won the lottery?" Numb, I replied, "No."

After the presentation of the symbolic check, we left the stage; one reporter was reporting our story on live TV, telling the viewers that the lucky winners of the Missouri Powerball were social workers with the Department of Social Services, Child Support Enforcement. Suddenly, I snapped out of my daze and shouted out loud, "Not anymore!" Everyone laughed.

Those words would be quoted in the newspapers and on the Internet. After taking more pictures, celebrating, and doing one-on-one live interviews, I left and went home. I did not go to sleep until late that night. That night and for the next week, our story was all over the local and national news. The news stations reporting the story included CNN, HNN, Fox, ABC, NBC, KMOV, and KPLR. Our windfall made news in every state. I was informed by my former office manager that a popular morning television show wanted to do an interview with us. We had to be at work early so that anchor person could conduct an interview.

Star struck, I arrived at work early for the interview. No one but the security guard was present. When my coworkers began to arrive, they heard that I had come to work early for an interview. They thought I had lost my mind. One former coworker came into my cubicle and asked me if I was all right. She reminded me that I would have to be more careful of whom I met and where I was. She then asked me if I knew who I was. She did not want anything bad to happen to me. I had not lost my mind. I found out later that the interview had been canceled.

My former coworker was partially right. I was in shock, and that shock would last for two years.

Chapter 7

SECURITY PLEASE

You would be surprised how many people try to use you when they find out you have money.

You see, I did not resign from my job immediately, because I would not receive my share of the lottery money for thirty days. Payment from my winnings was wired into an account and then transferred to the investment company I had hired to manage my money.

Once I hired the financial management company, my money was invested in stocks and bonds. I also had to decide how much monthly income I could live on and which day of the month I would receive that income. That income would come from the interest my investments earned.

When I finally received the paperwork from the Lottery Commission so I could wire my lottery winnings into my account in May 2006, I was very disappointed. As I said earlier, you do not get as much money as you think you are going to receive. Do not get me wrong; I am grateful for what I did receive. But what is hard to deal with is all the speculation as to how much money I actually have.

The truth is no one knows, but me. Each Lucky 13 Missouri Powerball Winner's winnings are different. We all invested our winnings differently. Sometimes the news media, with all its good intentions, can hype things up, make it out to be more than it is.

Like I said, when you win a lottery, people speculate about how much money you have without knowing the facts. Then they expect you to become their personal ATM machine. The truth is this: it is none of their business what you have. People will try to pull all kinds of scams and devise methods to unlawfully get your money. Always have an attorney or two who will watch your back. That is for your protection. Also, it is best to hire an estate planning attorney who will protect your assets.

Chapter 8

WELCOME NEW LIFE

After the public found out that I had won the lottery, many of my former clients and coworkers from other branches of the state and judicial system called me at work. They were not asking for money; they were congratulating me and wishing me the best. I will miss working with them.

On the flipside, I was also overwhelmed with less-well-intentioned people. I felt as if all hell had broken loose, starting in the month of April 2006 when my winning the lottery was publicly announced. People were coming out of the woodwork asking for money. Total strangers faxed letters to my job asking for money, and I had to screen my telephone calls at work because strangers were calling and asking for money. I had complete strangers coming into my job soliciting me for money and trying to interest me in business opportunities. They didn't just come to my job; people showed up at my house asking for money. I had people who felt that I should take care of all of their woes by paying for everything they wanted in order for me to be a part of their lives. I was put in the position of always helping others when others would not help themselves. Because of their relationships with me, they felt that they were entitled to what was rightfully mine.

Even if you consider helping people out, you should never give away your money without checking out their story first.

There was one woman in particular whom I had known for many years. Although we had not spoken in a few years, when she found out that I had won the lottery, she came over to my house. She told me that her real estate taxes were two years behind. She claimed that if I did not pay her taxes, she was going to lose her house. Something within me did not believe her, so I checked out her story to see if she was telling me the truth. When I looked up her address on a public website to verify her story, I found out that her taxes were not due. She had lied to me. Because she had lied to me, I decided to show her that I was no fool. I printed out the page that clearly showed her that her taxes were not due and mailed it to her. That was the last time I heard from her.

I decided it was time to set my resignation date. I chose to resign in May 2006.

In May, I finally received the paperwork from the Lottery Commission stating that my winnings could be wired into my account. After looking at the actual winnings versus the projected winnings, I was a little disappointed. As I said earlier, because of the taxes they take out before you get your winnings, you do not get as much money as you thought you were going to receive. Do not get me wrong; I am very grateful for what I did receive, but after all the speculation from individuals as to how much money I would receive, I was expecting much more.

The truth is no one knows how much money the Lucky 13 received. Each Lucky 13 Missouri Powerball winner's winnings were different because we all invested our winnings differently.

Chapter 9

My Aspiration

As a lottery winner and a mother, one of the first things that I did with the windfall of money was to secure it. I wanted to make sure that when I died, the money would pass down to the next generation. Also, I wanted to help my children financially by providing them with the important things in life they needed—not wanted. For example, I made sure that my grandchildren had college funds set up so that their college tuition would be paid.

People were excited. They wanted to know who I was. They had many questions about my life. I remember doing a television interview in which I was so overwhelmed that I couldn't complete it. At that point, my whole life was overwhelming. I did not share information with people regarding what I did for my family. I felt the information was personal. I did not want to harp on the fact that my children and I had had plenty of hard times. There were times when I was on food stamps. That was nothing to be ashamed of. I remember the day I was taken off food stamps and I had to depend on charitable organizations to help my family.

I will never forget the days when in order to feed my children I would go to a particular organization for food. This organization would give me a month's worth of food, toiletries, and the like, faithfully every month. They also helped me pay my utilities even though I had a job. I did not forget about that organization after I won the lottery. It was a blessing for me to be able to donate back to that organization as well as other organizations.

However, my major quest in my life was simply to prepare my children to have an easier life than I had had. I arranged it so that they would have nice futures, because that is what a mother does.

Chapter 10

Hollywood Comes to Town

I often reminisce about the day, before I resigned from my job, when I was informed by my office manager that some actors from California had received permission to come to the office to meet with the Powerball Lottery winners. The actors were considering producing a reality show about us. I was excited, nervous, and in awe. I wanted to know who these actors were!

My jaw dropped later that day when we met them in the conference room because I had had no idea one of my favorite actors would be standing in that room. They introduced themselves—as if I didn't know who they were. Please! They wanted to know if we wanted to film a reality show. After we asked them a dozen questions, we told them we might be interested. They then asked us if they could shoot the pilot that day. After they shot the pilot, which consisted mainly of questions, they asked for our telephone numbers and e-mail addresses. They told us that they would get back to us.

After they sold the ideal for the reality show to the network, they arranged to have a dinner party for us. They encouraged us to bring our friends and family. I thought it was a good idea; I eagerly accepted the invitation and asked my sisters to join me. Once we arrived at the restaurant, we took pictures and were introduced to the crew who would be filming the show.

I knew I was taking a chance when I signed the contract. At the time I did not care—or so I thought.

Chapter 11

LIGHTS, CAMERA, ACTION

The filming started in December 2006. I was on camera for approximately eight hours a day for twenty days. Those days of filming my life were interesting. Every day was a new adventure for me. I did not feel too overwhelmed.

Throughout the filming, the crew was very professional and patient with me. Every day, I was given an assignment by the lead cameraman, who managed and orchestrated the reality show. I was asked to pick a store of my choice to buy Christmas decorations. I choose Garden Ridge because I like the huge selection and variety of decorations they have.

When I arrived at the store, the crew asked me to wait in the car so they could get the store manager's permission to film. They also had to get consent forms signed by the customers and staff members who would be filmed in the store and be a part of the reality show. If they shot customers who did not consent to being in the show, they blocked their faces out.

So there I was, talkative and excited. People were following the camera crew, wondering what was going on. I heard the staff of Garden Ridge excitedly telling people that the camera crew was filming a reality show.

Each day, it was a different angle or story line that producers wanted to project as part of my life. I was asked to donate to a charity for the reality show, but I chose not to donate to a charity on camera, because I already donate to charities on a regular basis. Not really understanding what was happening, I did not go with the flow because I felt how much and to whom I donated money was a private personal matter. I did not want to have my donations filmed.

I have helped individuals to obtain things they were needed, such as cars. I've paid their utilities, bought food, helped to pay for furniture, and helped with funeral expenses. I remember a young lady who was a victim of a crime. I was told that she got into an altercation with a man and he knocked some of her teeth out by throwing a bottle at her mouth. When I met the young lady, I witnessed for myself the damage to her mouth. I felt sorry for her because from my understanding she did not have insurance, so I paid my dentist to fix her teeth.

I could have asked the people who received monetary help from me to replay the scene for the camera, or go to charities I have personal relationships with to let the cameras film me making donations. I chose not to. That was a mistake.

Chapter 12

CONTROVERSY IGNITES DRAMA

One of my most embarrassing moments while filming the reality show was when my son and I had an argument. I was disgusted with his behavior and I threw him out of my house. Although we were not on camera when the argument ensued, we had the microphones on. I knew there was a chance that this argument would be recorded, but had no idea that it would be edited into the show. I love my son, but I am from the old school. Do not raise your voice to me. Do not be disrespectful. In my opinion, the reality show made my son look like an unemployed want-to-be rapper. The truth is my son has worked for years at the same job. He works nights. He is a supervisor. I allowed him to temporarily move in with me so he could get on his feet. The move was supposed to be just that—temporary. I did my job and raised him. He went to college, and he is a grown man. My job is done. Our communication went haywire during the taping of the show.

Truth be told, when it comes to my son, I am the in-your-face; tell-it-like-it-is mama. I was not going to back down and let my son disrespect me in front of company. In reality, we disrespected each other, and the argument could have been avoided. But he had to leave my house. We needed to cool off.

A few days later, one of my favorite camera men, Dan (with whom I still talk today), devised a way for my son and me to make up. He had my son call me on the phone and invite me over to the house where he was now living. We made up and he showed me the studio where he makes music. I was impressed, but when the show aired, it appeared I was not supportive of his work.

The truth was that my son had been into music since he was a teenager. He even received a full ride—music scholarship—to a well-known university. He was in the university band and even became their drum major, but because of some problems, he did not finish his degree. When I won the lottery, my wish was for my grown children to get their degrees. I offered to help pay for their education. That is what I wanted for him. That was my disappointment with him. Not about his rap career, but about college. Cut and paste. He is a bright, smart young man and hopefully he will complete his degree.

Chapter 13

WAKE-UP CALL

As if the drama with my son were not enough, another drama occurred. This one I did not see coming. I was disappointed with the finished product from the reality show. In my opinion, the show focused on and highlighted problems, making my relationship with other family members appear to be dysfunctional.

The controversy shown was embarrassing. I had to live though it. What I saw from the show was jealousy, lust, and greed. I felt I had been raped and stabbed in the back by certain family members—people I had personally invited to be part of that reality show. Once again, you have to understand that this show was filmed in December 2006, but did not air until December 2007. Imagine the people you love appearing on television making comments about you that make it seem as if they do not love you.

Imagine how you would feel if they portrayed you badly, if they portrayed you as a selfish, greedy person. This was not the truth. Once again, I reiterate, controversy sells stories. After I saw the show and heard what they said about me, we did not speak for a year. I knew financially what I had done for them. That was not on the show. When we finally spoke, they told me that while filming the reality show they were asked questions that they answered. They claimed that they had no idea that their answers were going to be portrayed in a negative way on the show. They also explained that the questions they did answer were taken out of context. That reality show was an experience in my life. Even today a few people do not like me because of that reality show. Who cares? Cut and paste—it was just a reality show.

As much as I would have liked to have all the friends in the world, the truth is that I had a wake-up call. I realized that I could not trust everybody and all the money in the world could not buy friends or friendship. Also I learned that if you start your relationships off giving huge gifts, you have to continue doing that, because if you change, it will cause problems. My solution to the problem was to put a limit on my gifting. I had to change the way I thought, the way I evaluated people and situations. I am not a follower, but a leader. I learned to be around positive people. I have also learned to live a less stressful life by gravitating toward the positive things in my life.

Chapter 14

LIFE GOES ON

Another reason I was disapppointed when I saw the show was that most of my friends and daughters who had participated in the reality show did not make the final cut. They were interviewed and filmed by the cameramen. Those that did not make the final were the ones who were actually happy for me and wanted to be a part of the reality show. They were disappointed when they saw that they were not on the show. The many activities I participated in were filmed by the camera crew, but unfortunately, did not make it on the final show, because they were cut.

A brief flash was shown on the show when I gave a noon-time Christmas luncheon party in December 2006 for my former coworkers. I had food catered and gave everybody a gift. The camera crew interviewed my former coworkers who wanted to be interviewed. We all had a good time at the luncheon. It felt good being with them. That luncheon actually put me in the Christmas spirit.

We all know that controversy and drama sell. There was plenty of drama on my show. You take the good with the bad. I had no control over the people who made the decision of what made the final cut. The network knows what sells and how to run their business.

On the flip side, I really loved how the show ended; how despite what adversities my family and I experienced, we were able to come together as a blended family for Christmas dinner in the spirit of love. My son dedicated a beautiful song to me in which he expressed his appreciation of my love.

This experience made me learn fast how reality shows work. On the other hand, I have received a lot of positive feedback and support from people who watched the show. I have received support from the media, relatives, and the elderly and huge shout-outs from young adults. This includes people who live in other states and saw the show. I was made aware of this when I traveled. People would recognize me.

Believe it or not, even after that experience of being on the reality show, the network the show aired on is still today one of the networks I watch.

Chapter 15

GIVING BACK

Every year in June, the Missouri Lottery Commission holds a three-day event called "The Millionaires' Reunion." Each year a different city in Missouri is chosen for the site of the reunion.

The Millionaires Reunion is not just for millionaires, but for anybody who has won a substantial amount of money in the Missouri Lottery. The reunion stimulates the economy by reserving rooms at the hotel selected by the commission, making purchases, and by giving back to the community, through volunteer work and donations. At this event, the participants have an opportunity to talk to other winners and find out what's been going on in their lives.

The Commission encourages and welcomes friends and families to participate in the reunion. When you reply to your invitation, you report the number of guests you are bringing, send in money for the T-shirt orders, and pay for the reunion activities you are going to participate in. You then call the hotel to reserve and pay for your room. Then you are set to go.

The reunion lasts three days. When we arrive to the reunion we have a "meet and greet." Then we eat dinner. It is usually during dinner when we catch each other up on what has happened in our lives in the past year. Mainly, with the exception of a few, we all have the same stories. We talk about where we vacationed and our investments and share information about friends and family. I found out the longer you have had your money, the better experience you have in life. I have also realized that new winners learn from those who won the lottery years ago.

What I love the most about the experienced winners is their wisdom. One piece of advice I have received from the older winners is not to associate with people you know are out to use you. They advised me that they do not have those kinds of friends. Real friends will respect you for whom you are and love you the way they did before you won your money.

Each year at the Millionaires' Reunion there is a different cause. We give back to the community by volunteering to help various causes. One year, we volunteered to work at a carnival for a private grade school for children with disabilities. Another year, we volunteered to do chores at an animal rescue shelter. We worked one year landscaping a client's yard for Habitat for Humanity, and another year packing and passing out food to clients at a food pantry in Jefferson City. Each of us really enjoys giving back to the community by not only volunteering to work, but also by donating money for worthy causes. We look forward to the reunion and giving back to the community with a positive spirit. None of the group members, whom I have learned to know and love, are stuck up or snobbish. They are very down to earth and caring. We like to have fun.

The last day of the reunion is educational. A representatve from the Attorney General's Office will meet with us. We are given a lecture and vital information on subjects such as scams, identity fraud, theft prevention, consumer affairs, and other information we need to know. The speaker will pass out brochures that have contact information in case we need to use them. This meeting also consists of a question-and-answer period. The meeting can last an hour. I have found that these meetings are very beneficial to me.

Chapter 16

THE REFLECTION

Looking back at my grown children, I know they went through the same daze that I went through when I first won the lottery.

It has been five years ago since I received the windfall and today we laugh at each other. We still are a mess. Man, if the cameras followed us around when we are on vacation, they'd have enough for several new reality shows. I try to take my family on a summer vacation every year, because as a family we need to do that. We need to get away and relax. I take family vacations with my children to make up for the times I could not afford to take vacations when my kids were young. What some families may do naturally on a yearly basis was my dreams come true: vacationing together.

How do I manage my money in order to do what I want to do without going broke? I have a monthly budget. I manage to save money from that budget throughout the year, in order to get the things I want paid in cash. Plus, I love to travel. I know one day I might not be able to, so I want to travel while I can. Living with lupus has taught me to live each day to the fullest.

I still communicate with a few of the "Lucky Thirteen." A few have moved out of Missouri to other states, but we still talk. One in particular, I am going to visit in the near future. I just have to make sure she is not away on vacation when I am ready to visit her. I look forward to traveling with the lottery winners. Am I happy? Yes I am.

Chapter 17

NEW LOVE

I have not let this windfall go to my head; I am still the same person that I was before winning the lottery. I am in a good relationship with a man who is very supportive of me. See, I always knew that God had a plan for my life, even at my age and stage in life. All I wanted was a good man in my life. I just did not realize that person would be someone from my past. I have known this person since 1968 when we were children. His cousin lived next door to my parents. When he visited his cousin's house, he would sit on her front porch and wave at me when I was outside playing. I had no idea he liked me. Other than the occasional party his family members would have to which my parents were invited, I was not around him. In 1978 when I graduated from high school, he asked my mother permission to court me.

We dated briefly when I was eighteen years old and he was twenty. I remember our first date was at Steak and Shake.

He went to church with me and was even baptized at my church. However, later on that year, we parted and he moved to Detroit, Michigan. We would not see each other again for many years.

In 2006, my fiancé, Charles, and his cousin James visited my father's house to inquire about me; my sister gave them my telephone number. Later that day, I received a phone call from James, with whom I had been friends for many years. He had moved from St. Louis and moved to another state, but had now returned to St. Louis. When he called me I was excited to hear from him because I thought he was still living out of the state. After we talked on the telephone, I invited him to my house. To make a long story short, James was partially responsible for getting my fiancé and me together.

When Charles and I did meet, he told me that he had always liked me. He told me that he had even attended my high school graduation. Of course, I did not believe him because I did not recall seeing him there. He then took out a picture from his wallet and handed it to me. It was a picture of me in my graduation robe, receiving my high school diploma from my principal. I was flabbergasted. Our friendship was renewed.

Many times, events occur in our lives that we cannot control, but we need to go with the flow. Charles was employed at Chrysler for many years, but due to Chrysler's closing its Fenton Plant, he was given an opportunity to attend school.

In 2010, Charles graduated from a school with a degree in Culinary Arts. He also has taken an advanced nutritional training course for disease management. He has learned how to prepare food using organic produce to manage various illnesses. We both have disabilities, but he is determined for us to live a healthy lifestyle through a nutritional change of life. We make sure we eat daily fresh fruits and vegetables. We cook using natural herbs versus seasonings. We try to live a salt-free diet. We even have a small herb garden and grow our own vegetables.

Chapter 18

CONTINUE LIVING

Life goes on and old scars heal. I now can laugh at myself while watching the DVD of Million Dollar Christmas. When I have out of town guests they will ask me to put on that DVD because they love to watch the show and they laugh at all who was on the show. Life has a funny way of turning around.

Wait! I forgot to tell you. A year before winning the lottery, would you believe I actually had a dream that I won the lottery? That was unbelievable.

It can happen to you; you can win! Winning the lottery can be a blessing for people and change their lives when they are down to their last hope.

On the flip side of the coin, sometimes it can be a curse as their lives change. Have you heard the phrase "Curse of the Lottery"? It is true. Many curses come with sudden wealth. Some people live above their means by living extravagant lifestyles and lose all their money, some get addicted to drugs and alcohol, some become victims of scams, and some may even gamble their money away. My curses were the shock and fear of the huge taxes I had to pay, but there is no worst curse than losing friends and family.

That choice is yours. If winning the lottery happened to you, how would it change your life?

My life has changed since winning the lottery. My life now is a lot better. It is a blessing. Unfortunately, there is a downside. I have asked myself this question many times: Is the downside of my life worth the wealth I have accumulated? My answer is yes! You get used to dealing with people. You teach yourself how to be around people without being around people. You focus on your goals and what you want in life. You keep a level head and a meek spirit. Most of all, be watchful and do not live above your means.

I now understand that money is not evil, but the love of money is the root of all evil. Part of that evil is envy, the sense of false power, and greed.

ABOUT THE AUTHOR

Sandra Hayes is a graduate of Columbia College where she received a Bachelor of Arts degree in Psychology. She also is a graduate of Webster University, where she received a Master of Arts degree in Human Resource Management and a Master of Arts degree in Educational Technology.

After working for many years for the Federal and State Government, she is now retired. She was born and resides in St. Louis, Missouri. She has many hobbies, including cooking, gardening, fishing, and traveling.

Made in the USA
Middletown, DE
03 March 2019